MONSTER POEMS

Written by Barry Buckingham
Illustrated by John Pickering

HENDERSON
PUBLISHING PLC
©1995 HENDERSON PUBLISHING PLC

The Gruncher

"Halloo!" said the big, hairy Gruncher,
With eyes on the top of his head.
He grinned at the cat
Looking juicy and fat;
"I shall have you for dinner," he said.

"Oh, help!" cried the cat, all embarrassed,
"I've just had a bath, and I'm bare!
So if you must stay,
Will you please look away,
For it's ever so vulgar to stare."

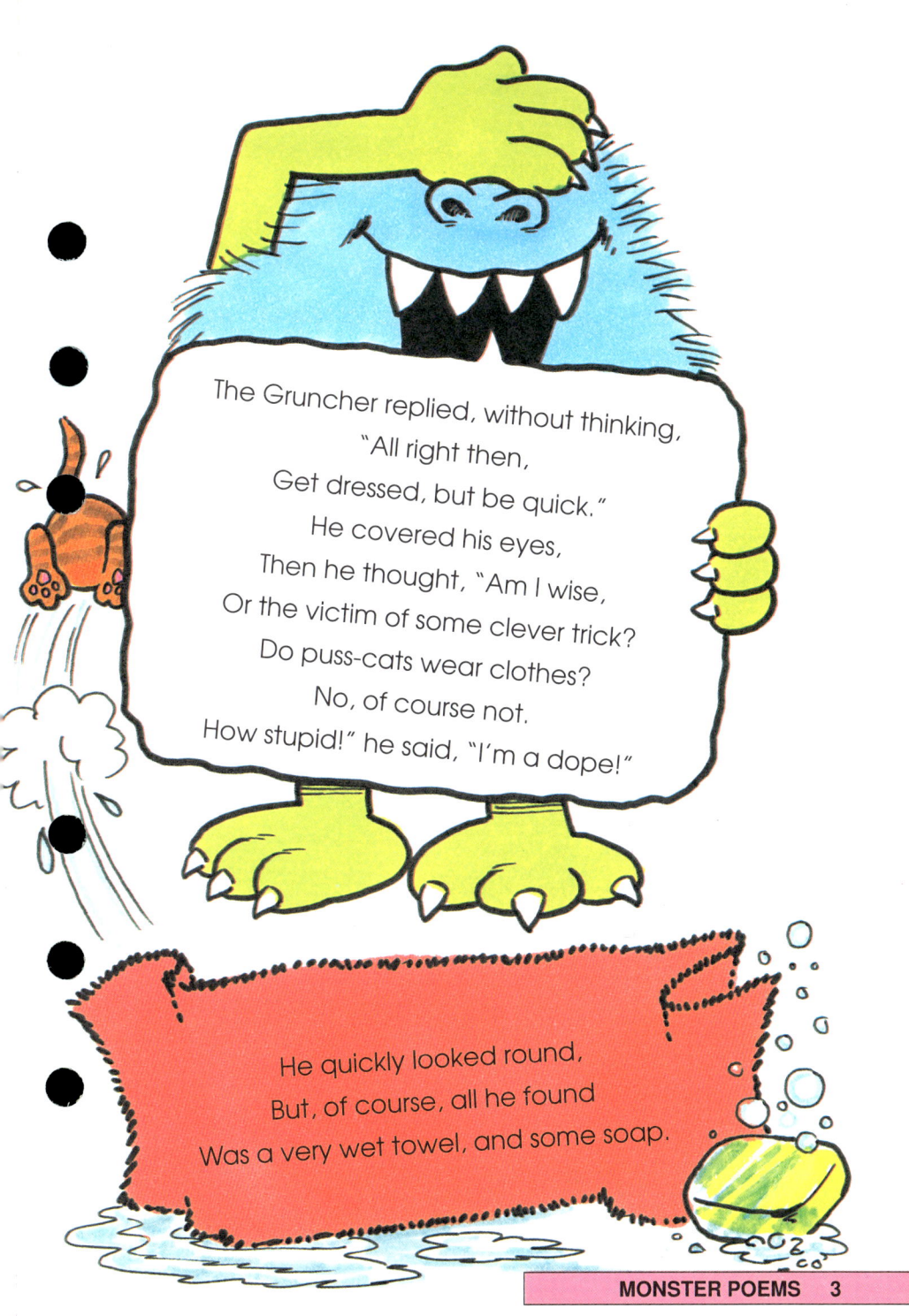

Brave Benjamin

As Benjamin walked home one day
With nothing on his mind,
A silent, dark-blue monster came
And followed close behind.

Four arms it had, four claws on each,
And four eyes in a line;
Its lower half was prickly,
Like a kind of porcupine.

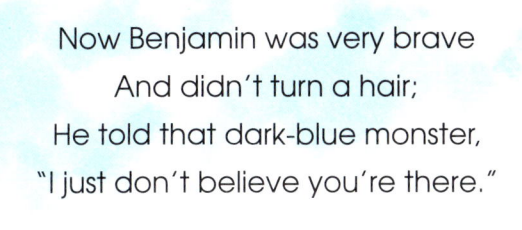

Now Benjamin was very brave
And didn't turn a hair;
He told that dark-blue monster,
"I just don't believe you're there."

The monster looked completely shocked,
And turned a lighter blue;
Then Benjamin stuck out his tongue,
As children sometimes do.

The gruesome thing went paler still,
And pulled an ugly face;
"You don't scare me," Ben told it,
"You're an absolute disgrace."

The monster went transparent
As it spluttered in dismay;
And then a breeze came wafting by,
And blew it all away.

MONSTER POEMS   5

The Magic Mountain

The mountain on Wallaboo Island
Looks solid and sombre and grey;
The islanders think it is magic,
And offer it fruit every day.

Now deep down inside it lives Norbus -
A great, shaggy hulk of a brute;
He looks like a big hairy sheepdog,
And welcomes those offers of fruit.

He likes to eat lemons in gravy,
And loves a banana skin flan;
He cooks massive tangerine dumplings
Which always roll out of the pan.

When smoke billows up from the summit,
The smell is of apricot roast;
Or Norbus has been very careless,
And frizzled his melons on toast.

If fractures occur in the mountain,
The islanders don't run and hide;
It's pineapple porridge, not lava,
That oozes from cracks in the side.

And if there's a massive explosion,
And boulders shoot into the sky,
They're just lumps of coconut popcorn
That Norbus is trying to fry.

The Blub

The Blub is fat, its eyes are small,
It has no arms or legs at all.
Like some great slug
it moves around,
And makes a slurpy,
sucky sound.

One day it thought: "To travel far
I need to buy a motor-car,
Then when I go on holiday,
I'll whizz along the motorway.

"What joy to go extremely fast,
With trees and houses flashing past,
Instead of creeping overground
All sluggish, with a slurpy sound."

And so it went, with head held high,
The fastest motor-car to buy;
But gracious me! - what did it find?
For Blubs, no cars have been designed.

It could not turn the starting key,
Or press the pedals separately,
And so - oh dear! Alas, alack!
It had to have its money back.

But never mind, the Blub's okay -
I saw it just the other day;
It's happy, making quite a breeze
When whizzing past on water-skis.

MONSTER POEMS

Little Monster

I went to Dr Muddleton
Who gave me lots of pills,
For I've been having tummy-ache,
And various other ills.
But I believe he's given me
Some pills I should not take;
They're pink, with yellow stripes on,
And I'm sure it's a mistake.

My face is going purple,
And my nose is cold and numb;
I've got a headache in my knees,
And toothache in one thumb.
My fingernails keep growing
Twenty inches every night;
Blue hair is sprouting from my ears -
I'm sure that can't be right!

Some other things have happened too,
But don't tell Mum and Dad;
They'll think I am a monster,
Not their darling little lad.
And now I'm really worried,
For I know I'll feel a fool;

How do I hide my swishing tail

When I go back to school?

MONSTER POEMS 11

The Octipod

The Octipod has problems
When he needs to buy some shoes;
He can't decide which arms are legs,
Although he looks for clues.
He surely has a few of each,
But cannot understand
Why some don't simply have a foot,
And others have a hand.

He needs at least two walking legs,
With four he'd go much faster,
But six would get all muddled up,
Which could be a disaster;
And if he thinks he has no arms,
But just eight simple legs,
How can he hold a knife and fork
When eating scrambled eggs?

12 MONSTER POEMS

The Abominable Snowman

At school we were told of the yeti,
Which lives in the peaks of Tibet;
It's called the Abominable Snowman,
But no-one has seen it - not yet.

They think it's a massive gorilla,
So won't make a lovable pet;
But all they have found are great footprints,
And no-one's got photos - not yet.

It walks in the snow with no boots on,
So must get its feet cold and wet;
I'm sure it would rather wear wellies,
But,
You can't get them that big - not yet.

14 MONSTER POEMS

Explorers have tried hard to catch it,

And carry it home in a net;

But surely it's clever and cunning,

For no-one's succeeded - not yet.

I'd tempt it down out of the mountains

With plates of baked beans and spaghetti;

But Mum says I must finish school first,

So,

I can't go and find it - not yeti.

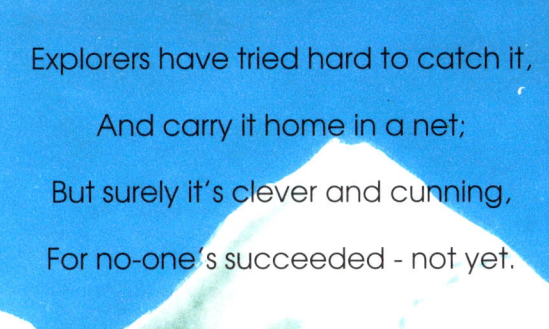

Dragon Groffen

In days of old when knights were bold,
And dragons fought them often,
There roamed a sad and lonely beast -
The gentle dragon, Groffen.

His daddy had expelled him
From the comfy family cave;
"And don't come back," he'd bellowed,
"Till you're fearsome, wild and brave."

As Groffen roamed unhappily
He paused to smell a rose;
Inside it was a bumble bee
Which stung him on the nose.

Fire jetted from his nostrils
As he rushed around in pain;
A woodman's cottage caught alight,
And then a barn of grain.

He flattened seven fields of corn,
And terrorised a town;
Then roaring like a hurricane
He knocked two castles down.

His daddy bellowed, "Come home, son,
I made a dreadful error;
I thought you were a softie,
But you really are a terror."

Night Beastie

Last night outside I wandered,
For I could not sleep at all;
I sat down in the darkness
On a seat against the wall.

Then suddenly a head appeared
Upon a scaly neck,
And then a dragon's body -
Ooh! I felt a nervous wreck!

The beasty stared with blazing eyes,
And stretched its fearsome claws;
It said, "I'm mighty hungry,"
And it snapped its toothy jaws.

I spluttered, "Just t-take whatever
Things y-you desire."
"I'd love some dolly mixture, please,"
It gurgled, breathing fire.

I only had some jelly beans,
So gave it three of those;
"How kind you are," it burbled,
Puffing smoke rings from its nose.

Next moment it had vanished,
Though it could be back tonight;
It's gruesome and it's ghostly,
But it's ever so polite!

Shy Zoozy

Big Zoozy lives high on a hilltop,
Alone among bushes and trees;
She eats lots of fir cones and conkers,
And honey from bumbly bees.

Her fur is all golden and silky,
With just a white patch on one paw;
Her tail has a knot in the middle,
And whiskers hang down from her jaw.

But no-one has seen much of Zoozy,
For though she is big, she is shy.
So when she hears people approaching
She hides until all have gone by.

But Zoozy gets ever so lonely,
And what she wants most is a friend;
A boy or a girl who is kindly,
And won't make a din,
Or offend.

So if you go up to the hilltop,
And gently call: "Zoozy! Coo-ee!"
Her head might pop up from the bushes,
Or peep round the trunk of a tree.

But if you are clumsy and thoughtless,
And whistle, or bellow and wail,
She'll panic, and rush through the bushes,
And all you will see is her tail.

MONSTER POEMS 21

The Dub-dub Bird

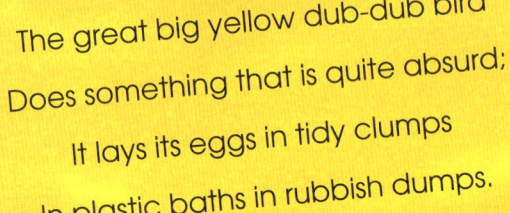

The great big yellow dub-dub bird
Does something that is quite absurd;
It lays its eggs in tidy clumps
In plastic baths in rubbish dumps.

Alas, some eggs get badly cracked
When other things on top are stacked,
But some hatch out, then dub-dub chicks
Go strutting round on legs like sticks.

They feed on rubbish in the dump,
And soon grow very large and plump,
Then each one hunts, when fully grown,
To find a bath to call its own.

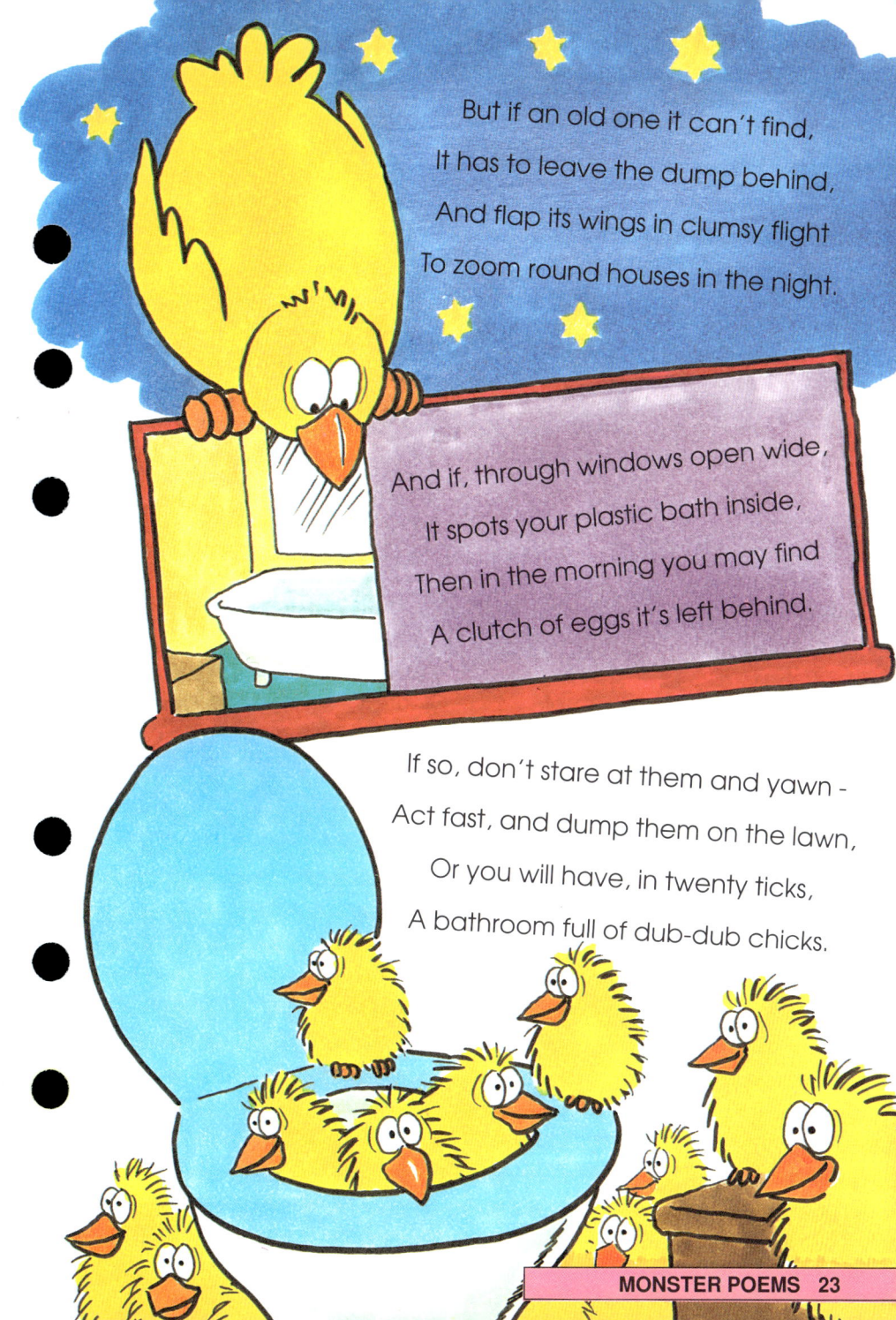

But if an old one it can't find,
It has to leave the dump behind,
And flap its wings in clumsy flight
To zoom round houses in the night.

And if, through windows open wide,
It spots your plastic bath inside,
Then in the morning you may find
A clutch of eggs it's left behind.

If so, don't stare at them and yawn -
Act fast, and dump them on the lawn,
Or you will have, in twenty ticks,
A bathroom full of dub-dub chicks.

MONSTER POEMS   23

Nessie

When up in Scotland I confess
I love the beauty of Loch Ness,
Where Jock,
With powered boat so nifty,
Takes me out for five pounds fifty.

But there today I had a shock.
"I'm charging ten pounds now," said Jock.
For he's become a rowing-boater -
Nessie's got his outboard motor.

Trouble from the Rubble

A bullying beastie called Zida
Was big as two barrels, and scary.
She looked like a spider
Did Zida,
With legs that were long,
thin and hairy.

In derelict houses she cowered,
And sprang out when
someone came near;
A very good hider
Was Zida -
She'd soon have you
quaking with fear.

26 MONSTER POEMS

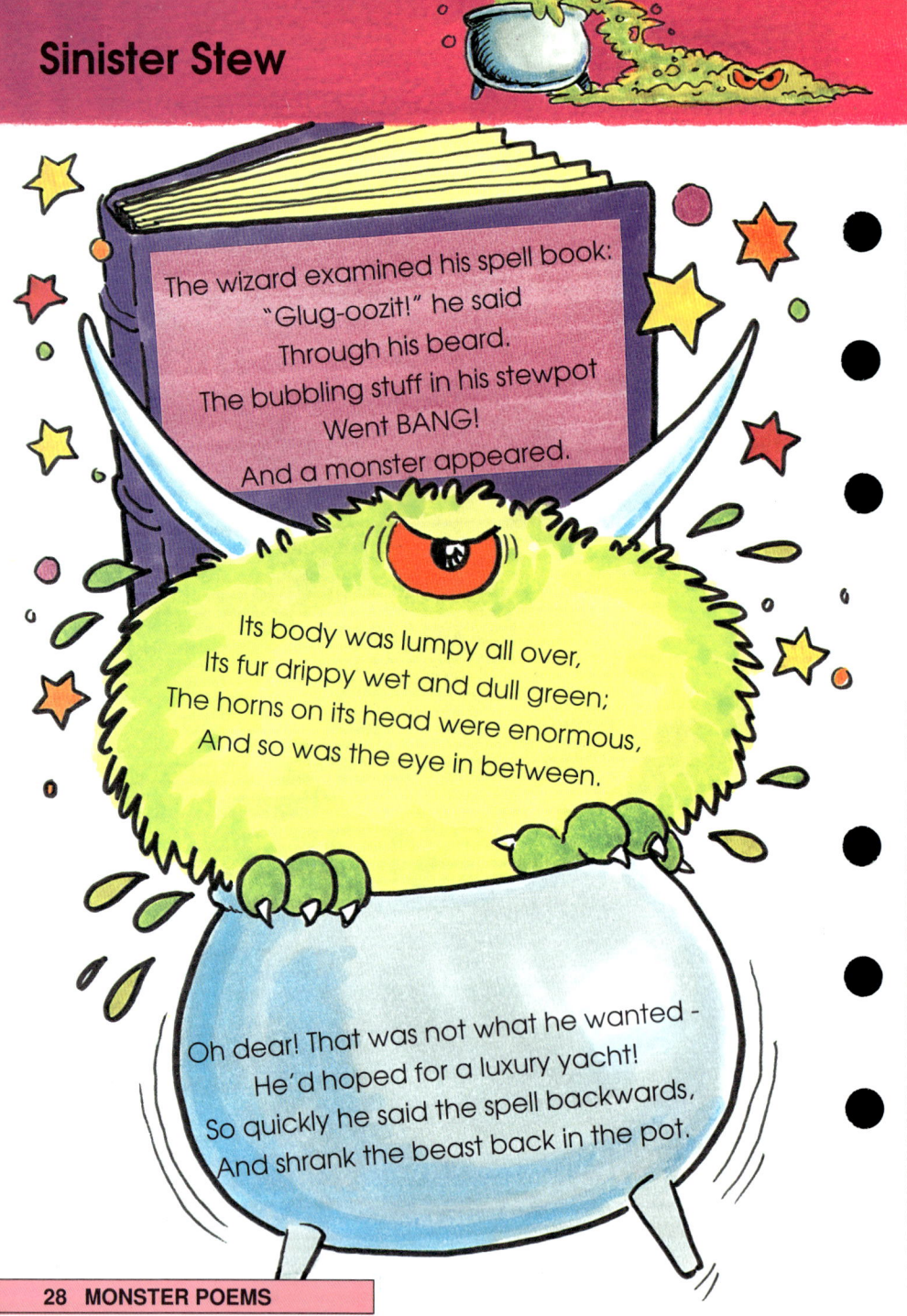

Oh, Daddy!

They picnicked in a meadow,
By an oak tree on a hill;
The day was warm, the food was fine,
And all went well until...

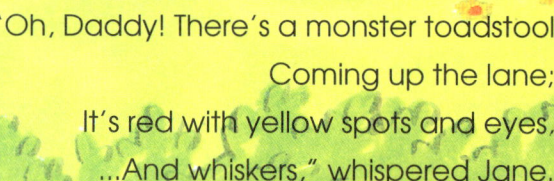

"Oh, Daddy! There's a monster toadstool
Coming up the lane;
It's red with yellow spots and eyes,
...And whiskers," whispered Jane.

"And has it got a silly hat,
And big ears?" Daddy laughed,
While Mummy said, "Now eat your crisps,
And don't be talking daft."

30 MONSTER POEMS

"But, Daddy, it's enormous,
And it must be near the car."
Said Mum, "Have a doughnut -
What a funny girl you are."

So Jane kept quiet
And said no more,
And spot on five o'clock
They packed up all the picnic things,
But then they had a shock.

Their new car had a dented roof -
What was the explanation?
Said Jane, "It was the toadstool giant
From my imagination."

The Very Rude Monster

A monster came on Monday
Like a great grey dinosaur;
It stood outside on four thick legs,
Its neck thrust through my door;
With eyes the size of saucepan lids,
It peered where it was able,
Then opened wide its great big mouth
And gobbled up my table.

On Tuesday it was back again
To see what it could find;
It swallowed up my TV set -
That wasn't very kind!
When Wednesday came it ate the fridge,
And all my store of food;
It never asks me if I mind -
I think it's very rude.

It stayed outside on Thursday,
And consumed my garden shed;
Today it's gobbled up my house,
With me still in my bed.
What's that? You don't believe me?
Have I told a fib or two?
Well, I do tell monster stories,
So perhaps it's not ALL true.

32 MONSTER POEMS